First published 1980
Third impression 1982
by The Hamlyn Publishing Group Limited
London · New York · Sydney · Toronto
Astronaut House, Feltham, Middlesex, England
© Copyright 1980
The Hamlyn Publishing Group Limited

Illustrations in this book have formerly appeared in *My Own Colour Dictionary,* and *My Own ABC,* both published by The Hamlyn Publishing Group.

ISBN 0 600 30489 2

Printed in Singapore by Tien Wah Press

My Little ABC

HAMLYN
London · New York · Sydney · Toronto

a

apple

apron

b

book

B

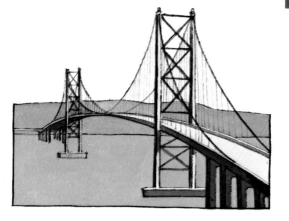

bridge

C

cake

C

cup

d

dinosaur

D

doll

e E

engine

f

F

flowers

g

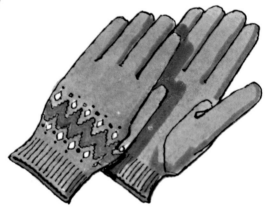

gloves

G

grapes

h

hammer

helicopter

i

ink

j J

jug

k

key

K

kite

leaf

lion

m

map

monkey

n

nails

necklace

orange

p P

parachute

q Q

queen

r R

rain

S

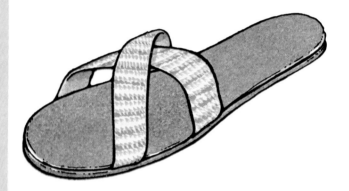

sandal

S

snake

table

T

tiger

U U

umbrella

van

W

watch

W

wheel

X X

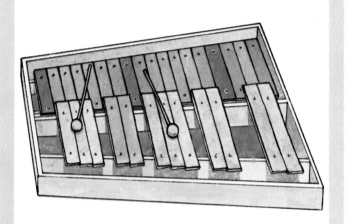

xylophone

y Y

yo-yo

Z

zebra

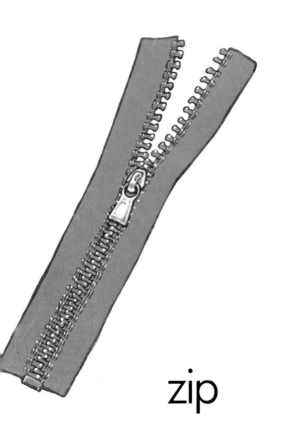

Z

zip